Moving On

Know where you're going and how to get there

Doug Franklin

Moving On
Know where you're going and how to get there

Copyright © 2012 by LeaderTreks

Published by LeaderTreks
25W560 Geneva Road, Suite 30, Carol Stream, IL 60188

Printed in the United States of America

ISBN: 978-1-934577-95-0

www.leadertreks.com
877-502-0699

Moving On

We've all sat at the dining room table while our parents, aunts, uncles, and grandparents stare us down and wait for the answer to their questions about our future. Sometimes the questions are open ended…

So where are you going to college? Will that internship look good on your resume? Have you applied anywhere yet? What are you going to study?

And sometimes the questions are a little more directed…

Your uncle is a doctor…maybe you could shadow him? Your grandpa was really athletic, he got a full ride scholarship to Rice University…have you tried out for the basketball team yet? When your sister got elected senior class president, it made all the difference on her college applications… have you thought about running for student government?

But ultimately, it comes down to…

What are you going to do with your life!!!!?

Insecurities about our future are something we all face, everyday, but they seem to be worse at times of transition; like when we are starting a new school year, or facing a graduation. So whether we are looking for a job, trying out for a team or in a serious relationship, transitions can force us to ask the hard questions about our future, and it can be daunting to try and find a clear answer.

This book is meant to help you sort through the clues God has already been giving you along the way. It's not meant to show you a Magic 8 ball view of your life, but simply to help you map out a picture of your future from the web of experiences, gifts and skills that God has already been weaving together in your life.

How Does This Book Work?

Thi book is about you. It's packed with illustrations, life stories from the Bible, and wisdom from people who have lived intentionally and have left impact. But each one of the stories is just an example of how someone read the clues that God was giving them in their lives. They uncovered their direction from His leading. This book is based on the following process:

> **Burden + Passion + Vision = Mission**

Each session takes you through a series of hard questions, discovery, and interaction with these clues. The things that break your heart (burdens), the things you love to do and that bring joy to your life (passions), and the things you dream about (vision), are all breadcrumbs to lead you toward life on a mission with Christ. By figuring out your mission, you'll be more equipped to handle moving on into your next transition.

Table Of Contents

Chapter 1
On The Road

Crystal was walking into unknown territory. Even after just graduating from a private college prep high school, she still wasn't that sure about college. After all, she was the first one in her family to even consider it. Her parents had put together money to make the private high school an option after seeing that the community school was going downhill. So Crystal went and ate it up. From dramas and sports to mission trips and retreats, she made sure that she took advantage of every opportunity. She even spent the summer right after graduation in the Dominican Republic, working at an orphanage. Crystal had gained a ton of experiences, and learned what seemed like a million things in high school, but one thing she was still clueless on was college.

Coming right off of her summer in the Dominican, Crystal had one week before she would arrive at her dorm. Everyone seemed to think this was barely enough time to get ready, so Crystal started right away. She emptied her duffle from her summer away, and began tossing in clothes until it filled up. She had lived the past 8 weeks out of that duffle, so to only fill it with clothes really seemed overboard. But hey, that was college right? Heading to the closet, Crystal yanked out a spare blanket and some sheets. She put those in a box, along with 3 pairs of shoes. She topped it off with a Ziploc bag containing her tooth-brush, shampoo and hairspray. Taping the box shut, she put it next to her duffle and looked around. She was ready. Why had everyone been making such a big deal about this? So Crystal soaked up her last week with her friends before loading her stuff in the car and making her trek into a new life.

Arriving at the dorm, Crystal was greeted by several RA's who were assigned to help the new students move in. Three of them came out to her car to put her stuff on a cart, and literally laughed when they saw the duffle and box. Crystal shrugged as one of the guys unloaded her belongings and they walked up to her dorm room to meet her two roommates, Michelle and Renee. They must have been super eager about college because they were long moved in, and when they showed her the room, Crystal began to realize how unprepared she was.

Michelle already had pictures up, and books on her bookshelves. She had slippers and matching towels, and her desk was completely maxed out in supplies. The radio (which Renee had brought) was playing, and Renee was trying to stuff the last of her clothes into the dresser. As Crystal went to see the bathroom, she saw that her roommates had brought their own plastic shelving that was set up and filled. It didn't take long for her to realize why everyone was so concerned about having only a week to get ready for college. Why did everyone need so much stuff anyways?

So Crystal filled two whole drawers of her dresser and made her bed, before she wandered down the hall to meet the rest of the floor. As the week went on, Crystal had a blast getting to know new people and a new city. But when school officially started, things changed. Everyone fell into routine and Crystal felt like a nomad. She was constantly borrowing things off Michelle's desk, from pens and paper to 3 ring binders. At night, when she couldn't fall asleep, she desperately missed her music collection and found herself trying to find something off Renee's bookshelf that would put her to sleep. When Crystal's friendships grew deeper, people would show her pictures and ask her about home and what she loved to do back home. This only sent her into a deep longing for her guitar, soccer cleats, and pictures of her family.

After the first couple weeks at school, Crystal sat on her bed surrounded by Michelle and Renee's worlds, and realized that nothing in this room or at this college resembled who she was. She felt lost. She had nothing to show for the first 18 years of her life, and she was tired of borriwng everything. It wasn't long before Crystal began making mental lists of what she would bring back the next time she went home.

It sounds ridiculous, but we often treat the next stage of our lives like Crystal treated college. It's a chance to be a minimalist, to purge all the things that have been taking up our physical and mental space. It's a chance to start over and be someone new, paving a new course that is in no way attached to our old journey.

Whether it's college, a career, or a new adventure, it's easy to think about the things we want to leave behind; what's hard is to remember the things we must bring with us. Things that resemble and remind us of who we are, where we've come from, what we love, and what we've overcome.

Crystal began college void of so many things that made up her identity. She had left behind valuable experiences and tools that had the potential to help her forge her own path. So instead, unequipped, she just tagged along on everyone else's journey. That's the danger of moving on to the next step in life without taking along the clues that God has given us so far. Through experiences, and a whole series of "likes" and "dislikes," God has been offering us pieces to the puzzle that can lead us into the adventure of a lifetime with Him. For years, He has been offering us breadcrumbs to show us the way and help us move on.

These breadcrumbs may not be huge events that stop us in our tracks. They may be small moments that trigger something deeper. They may be as simple as taking an inventory of your past experiences and deciphering what you want to keep as a part of your experience for the future. It may seem far-fetched, but if you absolutely love soccer and hate science, it may actually be some God-given clue to the next steps in your journey (not that it's an excuse to blow off necessary disciplines). The God that carefully knit us together gave us passions that would fuel our energy and focus.

Or what about those experiences that we are trying to forget about? You know, when your parents got a divorce two years ago, and college is your first chance to get away and escape the broken semblance of your family life. Maybe, that experience was a clue to the things that you are burdened for, and it would make you more equipped than most to encourage others in broken families. Another breadcrumb along the way.

Burden + Passion + Vision = Mission

The next pages in this book are designed to help you identify the things you can't and shouldn't live without, the valuables that ought to be the first things put into your suitcase. We're going to take a look at the different clues God has given you so far (burdens, passions, and vision) and use them to point you to the mission God has for you. Crystal took the minimalist approach to moving on, and in the physical sense, it's not all that bad. But to really hear God's voice and decipher the direction He has for you, we can't take the minimalist approach to packing for our journey with Him. There are clues we must pack, along with a compass to help us know where He wants us to go. If you have found yourself asking questions about what you should do with your future, take some time to really pour into the next pages, and more importantly, to train your ear to hear His voice along the way.

This book is divided into three main sections that guide you through these different areas:

Burden: What breaks your heart.
Passion: What brings you to life.
Vision: What God is telling you to do.

Through identifying and wrestling with these clues, this book will lead you through creating a mission statement that will help you navigate and walk confidently on this next part of your journey with Him.

> Many are the plans in a man's heart, but it is the LORD's purpose that prevails.
> Proverbs 19:21

Your Starting Point

One of the cool things about moving on is that it's not the start of your first journey. As you get ready for the road ahead, you are not starting from scratch. It's like beginning to train for a marathon after you've run a half marathon. You've already gone through a lot of training, your muscles are developed, your habits and your form have been established. You are much better prepared for starting this new phase than you were when you started your last journey.

Think about the last time you had to "move on" and really face a new road ahead. Maybe it was a literal move your family made. Maybe it was the start of high school, a new sport, job, or summer internship. Consider those experiences as part of the training. Spend a few minutes answering the following questions and identifying your strengths as you move on.

How are you different at this starting line than you were at the beginning of your last one? Standing at this starting line, I have way more knowledge, experience, and faith than I did at the last one.

What qualities, or character traits have you grown in and developed? (i.e. confidence, wisdom, peacemaking, humility)
I have developed more patience, confidence, wisdom, compassion, and humility.

What skills have you developed or grown in?
I have grown in listening and being relatable to others as well as traveling and using my words in front of many people.

How have you grown spiritually?

I trust god more than I ever have and I know that he is in control of my life! I have surrendered.

What solid relationships have you made or developed?

mason
ben
adam

These are some of your strong points. They are some of the things you can take confidence in as you start fresh on this new journey. When you are unsure or afraid, remembering these things will help you stay grounded. And these are also the first things to pack for moving on. So pull out that old duffel bag. It's time to get started.

Chapter 2
Burden

Burden

Ever wonder why, when we become Christ-followers, we don't go straight to heaven. Honestly, doesn't that seem like a good idea? Believe in Christ, and then go spend eternity with Him. We could probably avoid a lot of hurt and pain this way. The problem is, the rest of the world needs to know Him like you do. God has a plan to save the world…and that plan involves you. Think about what was going through the disciples' minds as they watched Jesus lift himself into the sky and speak one of the greatest missions ever heard. "Therefore go and make disciples of all nations."[1] I can imagine, as the fear built up in their throats, they were legitimately feeling like the weight of the entire world was on their shoulders. They were probably thinking "but Jesus, isn't that what you do? I can't do what you do." After all, if Jesus wanted to make disciples across the globe, it probably seemed like a good idea for him to stick around.

But no. He had a better plan. And that plan includes us. Equipped with the Holy Spirit, the Word of God, and direct access to Him, we are ready to embark on the journey of a lifetime.

If I was one of the disciples, I would have been shaking in my sandals as Jesus cast out his mission to me. This world is in desperate need of help. It is so broken, so corrupt, so hurting, so perverse that it's overwhelming to think that I'm part of the redemption solution. Me, a broken vessel that makes plenty of my own mistakes. But, somehow I am a part of the untangling process that can make paths straight and clear the way for people to come face to face with the One who can save them. The question is, where to start? What part of the knot do I begin untangling first?

Start Here - Go With Your Gut

Usually it's the last option, but here it's the first breadcrumb. We tell people to go with their gut when they've weighed all the options and truly can't decide. But when it comes to uncovering the map to the journey God has you on, your gut may actually be the first clue. It's the first because it tells you what burdens you. Burdens are the situations that compel you and draw you toward wanting to make a change. They are the things you can't ignore or simply turn your back on. They weigh you down and put a knot in your stomach. You can't turn your head from burdens, and they trouble you deep inside.

I was visiting a small group of college students one Sunday night, and everyone was talking about what they were going to do for spring break. Some were getting internships out of the way, some were going home, some were even going on mission trips, but I was shocked by one of the younger girls, Sarah, when she told me her plans. She was going on a mission trip, but not exactly what you think of when you think of a mission trip. She and a small team were going down south to a maximum security prison of death row inmates. For one week, her and her teammates were going to spend time with people who were sitting on death row and literally waiting to die. I think my jaw dropped. If there was ever a knot to untangle, here it was. My first reaction was "why?" and she was a little taken back because she couldn't think of why not to go. Her heart was burdened for the inmates, so when the opportunity presented itself, it was a no brainer. She had to go. It was all her heart would let her do.

Can you imagine the depths of despair this young college student would have to trudge through in order to bring even pieces of redemption into these inmates' lives? The terror, the guilt, the hopelessness, abuse, wretched sin. And this young girl was boldly going to bring hope where most people wouldn't even step foot. She was taking it seriously, "Go into ALL the world, and preach the good news to all creation"[2] ...yes, even death row.

Why? Because her heart was compelled when she considered the inmates' lives and saw the need for redemption. They were the last. They were condemned and considered by most to be beyond grace. There were few people who would even acknowledge them, let alone love them. Put simply, she was burdened. Of all the opportunities she could have taken for spring break, the choice was clear for her. Sarah had to do this because it was her gut reaction.

A burden is a powerful force in our lives. It causes us to make hard decisions and take very specific paths. Some people are burdened for those in poverty, some are burdened for the sick or the dying, others are burdened for addicts. The list of burdens seems endless, but no matter what your burden is, it's a force that will drive you down certain paths. And when you ignore a burden, it will tear you apart.

Burden Discovery

Take some time to answer the following questions in order to uncover what some of your specific burdens are. Remember, go with your gut! It's the most honest representation of what you're really feeling.

What's the first thing that comes to mind when you think about what your own burden(s) could be?

What are some things that break your heart?

When you watch the news are their certain stories that hit you?

If you were to reach out to someone, who would it be?

Are there certain age groups, or affinities that your heart breaks over?

What injustice or hurting people group are you drawn to?

Based on your answers to these questions what do you think some of your burdens could be?

This week, try and spend 15 minutes or so in a different news source every day. Try watching the local news one day, maybe CNN the next, and some online news sources the following, etc. Write down in the space below, some of the things that you felt burdened by as you watched the news?

*I can watch the news and be pretty desensitized by it. It seems like there's always a war, there's always a story of a murder or robbery, and there's always political tensions. But as soon as I hear the story of a kid being abused or abandoned, my heart breaks. I want to find that kid, help them, and work to get them in a loving home. Watching the news always helps me identify and motivates me to do something about the things I am burdened for.

What Breaks God's Heart?

As you look through scripture you cannot help but notice some trends. One such trend is that God has a heart for all his people. John 3:16 clearly states that He loves them, cares for them and sent his Son to die for them. Yet, when Jesus runs into a person that is either lost, broken, or last, he takes time to lend special attention. God has a special burden for these people. Here are some examples...

The Lost

"For the son of man came to seek and save what was lost." - Luke 19:10

It's pretty clear that God is burdened for the lost. Think about when Jesus called his disciples in the first place, promising to make them "fishers of men." Or the many parables he told about the lost sheep or the lost coin. What about the woman at the well, or even some of his last words as he spoke to the thief on the cross? There are countless stories of God's compassion for the lost, His soft heart, His care. God has a burden for the lost.

Who are the lost in the world today?

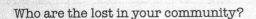

Who are the lost in your community?

The Broken

"Jesus went through all the towns and villages, teaching in their synagogues, preaching the good news of the kingdom and healing every disease and sickness. When he saw the crowds, he had compassion on them, because they were harassed and helpless, like sheep without a shepherd." – Matthew 9:35,36

Jesus healed the blind, the sick, the demon-possessed. He saw their situation beyond just physical healing, and into the healing of the heart. He knew the brokenness that was inside of people. He knew who was helpless, outcast, harassed, and he loved them. Remember the story of the woman who washed Jesus' feet with her tears and wiped them dry with her hair (Luke 7:36-50). She was broken, she was a sinner and she was shunned by the others in the room. Jesus, on the other hand, loved her deeply, stood up for her, and forgave her. God has a burden for the broken.

Who are the broken in the world today?

Who are the broken in your community?

The Last

"So the last will be first, and the first will be last." – Matthew 20:16

There's a great moment when the disciples get upset by all the people bringing babies and little children up to Jesus to have Him touch them (Matthew 19:13-15). After all, shouldn't Jesus be paying attention to the important people...the influencers, those of strong faith? But Jesus used the moment to teach the disciples how much He cared for the last. Even though they were just kids and society looked at them as non-contributors, they really mattered to Jesus. God has a burden for the last.

Who are the last in the world today?

Who are the last in your community?

Where Your Burden and God's Burden Intersect

The final step in figuring out your burden is to see how the things that break your heart and the things that break God's heart intersect. This will help you make sure your burdens have Kingdom weight and aren't simply emotions.

Go back to the Burden Discovery in page 12 and take a look at what your answers point to. Do your burdens line up with God's heart for the lost, the broken or the last? If they do, write down which one (lost, broken or last) each of your burdens correlate with.

Nehemiah's Burden

The story of Nehemiah is a great one. It's got all makings of a great movie. The heart of a champion, overcoming impossible odds. But it also is a really great example of taking on God's mission for your life. Nehemiah was a slave. He was part of the Jewish remnant who all got dispersed after their nation was destroyed around 600 BC. He was a displaced foreigner, and serving as a cupbearer to King Artaxerxes (cupbearer = the person who tastes the wine and food before the king eats it, so the king can be sure it's not poisoned). But God was giving him training and clues the whole time, for a great mission that He had for Nehemiah.

Sound familiar?

Read Nehemiah 1:1-4 and answer the following questions:

> *The words of Nehemiah son of Hakaliah: In the month of Kislev in the twentieth year, while I was in the citadel of Susa, Hanani, one of my brothers, came from Judah with some other men, and I questioned them about the Jewish remnant that had survived the exile, and also about Jerusalem. They said to me, '"Those who survived the exile and are back in the province are in great trouble and disgrace. The wall of Jerusalem is broken down, and its gates have been burned with fire."' When I heard these things, I sat down and wept. For some days I mourned and fasted and prayed before the God of heaven.*

What is Nehemiah's burden?

How can you tell that is his burden?

How does it correspond with God's burden?

After this, Nehemiah takes on what every other Israelite deems impossible. He actually gets a leave of absence from the king to go back to Jerusalem and rebuild the walls around the city. But not only does the king give him the time off, he also gives him all the supplies he needs, army officers and cavalry. So Nehemiah goes to Jerusalem and casts the vision for the people. Everyone joins in and begins the building process. Even when other nations begin making threats, Nehemiah stands strong and leads well. After only 52 days the walls of Jerusalem stood high and the nation was once again gathered. (just so you know, the walls of Jerusalem were not just some block walls, they were 4.5 miles around and almost 20 feet thick).

Nehemiah had a burden he could not deny. Seeing his people displaced and separated from God was too much. It broke his heart, and no matter what he did, he could not be satisfied until he did something about it. Like Nehemiah, your burden is a clue to a larger mission. Some burdens are greater than others, but they can all be breadcrumbs to lead you down the road as you move on.

Most importantly, don't leave your burdens behind (which will most likely lead to regret and frustration) but actually dive into learning more about what burdens you. Spend some time in research finding more information on the issues you are concerned about. Try to discover possible solutions to these problems and see if there are things you can do, even now. to help remedy the situation.

Chapter 3
Passion

Passion

In one of the greatest classic movies of all time, *Chariots of Fire*, Eric Liddell's life was put to the movie screen (If you haven't seen this movie, it's worth a rental). Eric was a Scottish runner, and qualified for the 1924 Olympics, but running wasn't all that he was about. Eric was also a devout Christian, and had a burden for the people of China and bringing the gospel to them. The "problem" was, he also qualified for the Olympics and truly loved to run.

The tension built between Eric and those who knew him best. His sister, confronted him about putting off his vision of bringing the gospel to unknowing people, and he responded with one of the greatest lines in the movie, "I believe that God made me for a purpose, but he also made me fast, and when I run, I feel his pleasure." And it was true; you could actually see it when he ran. As the finish line approached, he didn't focus forward and follow through; instead he would throw his head back and let his arms hang loose as he took in what could only be described as God smiling down on him.

Eric pursued running and trained hard for the Olympics. However, when he boarded the boat for the Olympics in Paris, he learned that the 100-meter dash (one of the races he had spent years training for) was taking place on Sunday...the Sabbath. Faced with pressure and even the urging of the Prince of Wales, Eric refused to run on the Sabbath, forfeiting the opportunity for an Olympic medal.

It made the worldwide news. Headlines across the globe focused on Eric's decision. From the top down, princes and kings, to the everyday man, the world heard about Eric's God. Eric had a passion for running, and when he honored God with it, he was able to reach more people with the news of his Savior than he ever imagined.

Eric's story doesn't stop there. Another athlete gave up a spot in the 400-meter race later that week. Eric took his place and went on to win a gold medal. And following the Olympics, Eric went on to China where he taught chemistry and English to peasants under harsh conditions, using it as an opportunity to share Christ. In the end, under the Japanese invasion of World War II, Eric died as a prisoner of war.

Eric Liddel was a hero of the faith. God made him unique, with experiences, burdens and passions that didn't always seem to fit together, but came together perfectly when he honored God with them.

What is Passion?

Passion is an important part of the formula when you think about a life mission and moving on. Passions don't always seem super spiritual, as much as they seem invigorating and motivating (like running), but they can still be breadcrumbs in the process of uncovering your road map. Passions are often the fuel that propels you forward on your mission. They can also be the sweet spot that brings you joy and connection with Christ.

So what is passion? Passion is more than an emotional connection with something or someone. It's an intense driving desire. It's something you love to do, and it stirs inside of you. It's what moves you, and it's what you're doing in the moments that you feel God's pleasure. Passions are what bring you to life.

Take some time to answer the following questions in order to uncover what you are passionate about. Remember, go with your gut! It's the most honest representation of what you're really motivated and inspired by.

When are the moments you feel God smiling down on you?

What could you do for hours on end and not get bored?

What do you simply love to do?

What are the things you find yourself looking forward to?

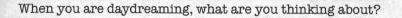

When you are daydreaming, what are you thinking about?

What can you always make time for?

Passion Comes from God

As Christ followers, the thing to know about your passions (when they really are passions and not lusts or idols) is that they come from God. God wired you uniquely to be energized and great at certain things. He didn't design and create you to live an unfulfilled life, He designed you with passions that will drive you and cause you to expand your ideas of what you are capable of. Tied together with your burden and vision (which we'll get to in the next chapter) your passions will propel you into actions that change you from just having a burden, to becoming a solution.

Passionate Paul

Take a look at Acts 17:16–34 and how God gave Paul passions that would increase his ministry potential.

While Paul was waiting for them in Athens, he was greatly distressed to see that the city was full of idols. So he reasoned in the synagogue with both Jews and God-fearing Greeks, as well as in the marketplace day by day with those who happened to be there. A group of Epicurean and Stoic philosophers began to debate with him. Some of them asked, "What is this babbler trying to say?" Others remarked, "He seems to be advocating foreign gods." They said this because Paul was preaching the good news about Jesus and the resurrection. Then they took him and brought him to a meeting of the Areopagus, where they said to him, "May we know what this new teaching is that you are presenting? You are bringing some strange ideas to our ears, and we would like to know what they mean." (All the Athenians and the foreigners who lived there spent their time doing nothing but talking about and listening to the latest ideas.) Paul then stood up in the meeting of the Areopagus and said: "People of Athens! I see that in every way you are very religious. For as I walked around and looked carefully at your objects of worship, I even found an altar with this inscription: TO AN UNKNOWN GOD. So you are ignorant of the very thing you worship—and this is what I am going to proclaim to you.

"The God who made the world and everything in it is the Lord of heaven and earth and does not live in temples built by human hands. And he is not served by human hands, as if he needed anything. Rather, he himself gives everyone life and breath and everything else. From one man he made all the nations, that they should inhabit the whole earth; and he marked out their appointed times in history and the boundaries of their lands. God did this so that they would seek him and perhaps reach out for him and find him, though he is not far from any one of us. 'For in him we live and move and have our being.' As some of your own poets have said, 'We are his offspring.'

"Therefore since we are God's offspring, we should not think that the divine being is like gold or silver or stone—an image made by human design and skill. In the past God overlooked such ignorance, but now he commands all people everywhere to repent. For he has set a day when he will judge the world with justice by the man he has appointed. He has given proof of this to everyone by raising him from the dead."

When they heard about the resurrection of the dead, some of them sneered, but others said, "We want to hear you again on this subject." At that, Paul left the Council. Some of the people became followers of Paul and believed. Among them was Dionysius, a member of the Areopagus, also a woman named Damaris, and a number of others.

Answer these questions based on the verses you just read and what you know about Paul in general.

What do you think Paul loved to do?

What are some of the characteristics of Paul's personality?

How was Paul able to use his passions to further God's kingdom?

Paul was passionate about learning and debating. He was highly educated, and a well mastered communicator. If he was in high school today, he would be captain of the debate team, and probably filling out law school applications. His love for debate comes out in his writings (take a look at Romans) and relationships all the time. The best part is that when Paul submitted his life to God and used his gifts and knowledge to honor Him, God used Paul's passions to develop him into one of the greatest missionaries the world has ever known. Paul went on to write twelve books of the Bible and brought countless people to faith. This is the power of our passions when they come from God and are used to honor Him.

The world is full of boring, unexciting Christians. It's full of people who have mastered the language of Christianese, and artfully put together wardrobes that match the Christian culture we have created around us. We have artists and colors that we call our own, and even have harmonious ways we deliver the news on our radio stations. We have built a Christian Culture empire in which admission is based on a set of rules rather than the faith that pours from your heart. In fact it's easy to pick out who the new believer is because they speak openly and bluntly about struggles and sin without hiding it in a prayer request. This world is full of boring Christians who rigidly follow an unspoken system of do's and don'ts. I don't know about you, but I don't want to live in that world.

C.T. Studd put it this way, "Some wish to live within the sound of Church or Chapel bell; I want to run a Rescue Shop within a yard of hell."

The truth is, you are going to live forever. You are going to live for all eternity, and the first 70 years or so are going to be here on earth. Why play it safe? Why make sure you fit into a fake mold that makes it look like you're a great Christian. Why not choose to spend these first 70 years taking risks and putting into action the passions and the gifts that God planted in you.

The author of Hebrews desperately wants to motivate people to get up and run on this journey with Christ. He goes into great detail, telling the stories of those who've gone before us. The stories of faith heroes who never settled for playing it safe, but passionately pursued their God and lived out the redemption story in radical ways on earth. Hebrews 11 is known as the Hall of Faith, telling the story of incredible followers of God who *"conquered kingdoms, administered justice, and gained what was promised; who shut the moths of lions, quenched the fury of the flames, and escaped the edge of the sword;..."* The author wanted to inspire Christ followers to live differently. To not be caught in the tangles of culture, but to run after Christ and His mission. Hebrews 11 leads us into these verses of motivation...

> *"Therefore, since we are surrounded by such a great cloud of witnesses, let us throw off everything that hinders and the sin that so easily entangles, and let us run with perseverance the race marked out for us. Let us fix our eyes on Jesus, the author and perfecter of our faith who for the joy set before him endured the cross, scorning its shame, and sat down at the right hand of the throne of God."*
> — Hebrews 12:1-2

Passion is a key part of our Christian faith and our journey. It isn't something to be stuffed away and covered up, it's something to utilize and fuel your mission. You are going to have to decide in your life, will you passionately follow Christ? Will you join Christ only in lifestyle or will you join Him with your heart? It sounds harsh, but by the time you graduate college, it's probably too late to make that decision. Living with God's passion in your heart allows you to live life to the fullest. Jesus said in John 10:10, "I have come that you may have life, and have it to the full." Living with passion is living as you were meant to be.

Passion Survey

Flip over to page 62 and take some time to go through the Passion Survey.

Burden + Passion

Sometimes, our passions and our burdens intersect so closely they are interchangeable. You might be passionate about children's ministry and burdened for children, or passionate about justice and burdened for the oppressed. This can be a really good thing so don't worry if your burden and passion seem almost the same. It's great when what breaks your heart and what inspires you are so easily linked. It makes moving on that much more clear when it comes to the hard decisions you will face.

If your passions don't seem to line up really well with your burden, that's okay too. God has uniquely designed you and has a plan for you. For Eric Liddel, running was one of the things he was passionate about, but it didn't seem to fit with his burden, or even his vision. But God had a very intricate plan to use Eric's passion to reach across the world with the message of the Gospel, something that was true to both his burden and his vision.

The key for us is that whether our passions make sense and fit well into the equation for discovering our next steps, or if our passions seem to be the oddball in the equation; we must always focus them on honoring God. The dangerous side of passion is it can quickly become an idol we put before God. Eric Liddel could have easily turned running into an idol. The amount of training and focus it took, not to mention the fame and glory that come from Olympic medals, could have easily taken something that was God's gift to him and made it something greater than God himself. But when put to the test, Eric stood firm in his devotion to God. He was willing to sacrifice running in order to honor God.

Take a look at your top 3 answers from the Passion Survey, and ask yourself the following questions.

How do I (could I) honor God with these things that I'm passionate about?

Could any of these passions become idols in my life?

How do I keep myself from letting things I'm passionate about become idols?

It's very important to not only know what you are passionate about, but also to tap into it and make it a part of your life. The mission road can (and will) be hard at times, and it's at those times your passion will become the fuel that helps you overcome obstacles and carry on. In other cases, living inside of our passions can be a place of rest and connection with our Savior. The power of passion is not only vital in our walk with Him, but it can also be where you find the most joy.

Chapter 4
Vision

Vision

I can see clearly now the rain is gone.

I can see all obstacles in my way.

Gone are the dark clouds that had me blind.

It's gonna be a bright (bright) a bright (bright) sunshiny day

(1972, Johnny Nash, Epic Records)

If there was a perfect soundtrack for moving on...this would make the list for me. Can't you just feel it, driving down the highway with your windows down. Enjoying the first days of spring, and the last days of your Senior year. And just when it seems like it couldn't get better, that scratching sound rips through the radio and breaks up the song. Followed by the famous question that every adult you encounter has asked...so what are you going to do with your life? Where are you going to college? What are you going to major in? What do you hope to be? And it doesn't take long before the moving on experience gets deflated.

One part of my job often takes me on road trips across the country in the summer. I'm visiting mission sites, or encouraging staff who are leading trips. And one of the routes I know really well is between Chicago and Hazard, KY. I've made this trip more times than I can count; it starts out as a straight shot down the flatlands of the Midwest, and just past Louisville, it turns into beautiful mountains. As you get farther into the mountains the roads get more narrow and wind quite a bit, so the thing you've got to watch for are coal trucks around the bends. In many cases, you can barely fit two cars, let alone a giant coal truck (that doesn't exactly have the capacity to stop on a dime) and a car.

So as the beginning of a recent summer rolled around, it was time for me to make that trip yet again. Two interns and I packed a van full of work project supplies and headed on the road. One of the things I love most about road trips is the time you get to build relationships with the people you're driving with. So we were talking and stopped for lunch at Chick-fil-A, then hopped back in the car with our milkshakes just as a thunderstorm was approaching. We figured it would pass, and we'd just drive right through it, but instead it hovered over us for the entire ride. As we made our way into the mountains, we went from lively conversation, to tense silence. We were all squinting our eyes and focused on the road. And the deeper we got into the mountains, the more we seemed to be crawling along. We'd pass under bridges where some cars had pulled over to wait it out, we'd stay far behind the trucks because their spray was blinding, and we never left the middle lane because the outer lanes were collecting larger puddles by the minute. The wipers were going as fast as they could, and the sound was adding to the intensity we already felt.

When we finally arrived at the team house in Kentucky, we rolled out of the van exhausted. The trip took 3 hours longer than expected, and I don't think the muscles in our shoulders had relaxed since lunch. We stretched our legs out as we walked, and emptied out the van as quickly as possible so we could relax and grab dinner. When you think about it, all we did was sit in a van all day and eat. But we were so tired by 8:00 that night that we could barely keep our eyes open. Why? Because we spent most of the day without clear vision. When the storm came, driving became a lot harder. Staying clear of semi trucks loaded with coal became stressful. Avoiding the rivers of water that were forming on the roads took all our concentration. When it comes down to it, it's stressful and exhausting to live without clear vision.

Without vision, we are constantly on the defense, waiting to see what obstacles are coming and how much they will take from us. Without vision, we are so focused on damage control that we miss out on the depth of relationships around us. And honestly, living without vision makes it so we can't reach our potential. In essence, we aren't the most effective or impactful when we can't see clearly.

Think back to your burdens and your passions. There are things that are welling up inside you, compelling you to make changes in this world. Vision is the thing that helps us get there. Vision helps us make significant, intentional change in this world. Burden without vision is just a broken heart. Passion without vision is just a lot of fun. But vision is what brings meaning and kingdom potential to the equation. Without it, we may as well be driving the winding roads of Kentucky in a thunderstorm.

So What Is Vision?

Vision is what God's telling you to do. It's a calling to something greater than yourself. Vision takes into consideration your past, your gifts, and your unique experiences. It's something that started forming before you were born as God created you. It has been developing and growing with each experience. Vision is given by God.

When identifying your vision, there are several things to remember:

1. You probably will have more than one vision in your life. You may have a vision to be a doctor, or to serve a specific people group. But you may also have a vision to be a parent, or to coach a team. It's normal to have a few different visions that will take course over a long period of time

2. Visions may change. During this chapter, we're going to work on identifying what it is that you are aiming for, what you think God is telling you to do. Remember that as you grow and have new experiences, God may add new visions or callings on your life. Think of how many people have set up foundations for cancer research or disabilities because they grew that vision when they became close with someone who struggled with it. It may not have been the vision they set out to conquer originally, but it became just as important to them.

3. Not all visions encompass every burden and every passion. At different times and places, there are moments where we put into practice different passions and affect different burdens. That's okay. Much like Eric Liddel's passion to run didn't fit his vision of preaching the gospel in China, our passions may not always fit our vision. It shouldn't keep us from pursuing a vision that is God-given (as we see in Eric's case, God used both his passion and vision separately) and it shouldn't discourage us from not living out our passions or burdens. They may not all come together at the same time and same place, but they are all gifts from God that can be used by Him, and can help us with the decisions to make along the road.

With that being said, there are a lot of things to take into account when discovering God's vision for you. Some clues to this come through unique abilities and gifts that He's equipped you with. Other clues come from prayer and connection with Him. Over the next several pages we'll spend some time identifying how He uniquely made you and how you can practice listening to His voice in your life.

For we are God's workmanship, created in Christ Jesus to do good works, which God prepared in advance for us to do.
- Ephesians 2:10

Unique Abilities Profile

Take some time to go through the Unique Abilities Profile on page 76 and see how these abilities might be leading you toward a specific vision in life.

When you are finished, write down your top 3 Unique Abilities

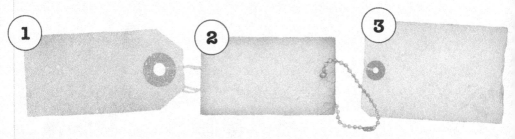

1   **2**   **3**

God gifted you for a specific role

Another way we are equipped for God's vision are through Spiritual Gifts. I Peter 4:10 says *"Each one should use whatever gift he has received to serve others, faithfully administering God's grace in its various forms."* Everyone who is a Christ follower has been given a specific Spiritual Gift. These gifts are so that we can all fulfill a role in the body of Christ. Since we don't all have the same gifts, we don't all fulfill the same roles. Your spiritual gifting is a large clue to your vision.

Spiritual Gifts Assessment

Take some time to go through the Spiritual Gifts assessment on page 82 to learn more about your gifting, what the Bible says about it, and how it plays out in your life. When you are finished, write down your top 3 spiritual gifts.

1   **2**   **3**

Connect with God

Unique Abilities and Spiritual Gifts play into our vision and can lead us down the road of discovering it; but most importantly, if you want to know what God's vision is for your life, connect with the One who holds it.

This is something that seems so basic, but it's probably one of the last things we tend to do. Many times, we go about making plans for our lives, and then we check in with God to ask him if He could help us out with it. It's easy to get in the habit of telling God what we need instead of asking Him what He has for us. He holds each day of our lives in His hands. If we really want to know what the vision of our future is, we should connect with Him regularly and listen.

Take a look at what David writes in Psalms about how deeply God knows us, knows our future and understands every unique thing about us.

Psalm 139: 1-18

> *You have searched me, LORD,*
> *and you know me.*
> *You know when I sit and when I rise;*
> *you perceive my thoughts from afar.*
> *You discern my going out and my lying down;*
> *you are familiar with all my ways.*
> *Before a word is on my tongue*
> *you, LORD, know it completely.*
> *You hem me in behind and before,*
> *and you lay your hand upon me.*
> *Such knowledge is too wonderful for me,*
> *too lofty for me to attain.*
>
> *Where can I go from your Spirit?*
> *Where can I flee from your presence?*
> *If I go up to the heavens, you are there;*
> *if I make my bed in the depths, you are there.*
> *If I rise on the wings of the dawn,*
> *if I settle on the far side of the sea,*

even there your hand will guide me,
your right hand will hold me fast.
If I say, "Surely the darkness will hide me
and the light become night around me,"
even the darkness will not be dark to you;
the night will shine like the day,
for darkness is as light to you.

For you created my inmost being;
you knit me together in my mother's womb.
I praise you because I am fearfully and wonderfully made;
your works are wonderful,
I know that full well.
My frame was not hidden from you
when I was made in the secret place,
when I was woven together in the depths of the earth.
Your eyes saw my unformed body;
all the days ordained for me were written in your book
before one of them came to be.
How precious to me are your thoughts, God!
How vast is the sum of them!
Were I to count them,
they would outnumber the grains of sand—
when I awake, I am still with you.

How well does God know you?

What does God think of you?

Do you think God has a plan for your life?

What do you think He believes your potential is?

Connecting the Dots

The next two pages in this book are empty. Either right now, or sometime today when you have a chance to get away and spend some focused time with God, write down what you think God might be telling you to do. Look back at your Unique Abilities and Spiritual Gifts, and ask God what direction and steps He wants you to take. Write down what you think are some visions for your life.

For some of you, this might be easy, and you might already have a clear view of your vision. But for others of you, your vision might seem more like driving in a thunderstorm. Regardless of where you are on the spectrum, connecting with God on your vision is a must. He holds it, He has the plans, and when we are in step with Him, we can attain it. Whenever we fall out of rhythm with Him we are in danger of finding ourselves in a thunderstorm. Besides that, our vision doesn't matter without Him. He created you, He ordained each of your days, He has a plan for you and a place for you in His Kingdom.

Reflect on these words from Paul, as you spend time connecting with God about your future.

> *"I want to know Christ and the power of his resurrection and the fellowship of sharing in his sufferings, becoming like him in his death, and so somehow, to attain the resurrection from the dead. Not that I have already obtained all this, or have already been made perfect, but I press on to take hold of that for which Christ Jesus took hold of me. Brothers, I do not consider myself yet to have taken hold of it. But one thing I do: Forgetting what is behind and straining toward what is ahead, I press on toward the goal to win the prize for which God has called me heavenward in Christ Jesus."* - Philippians 3:10-14

"Never be afraid to trust an unknown future to a known God."
–Corrie Ten Boom

If you really want to stay connected to Christ, consider making this a regular practice. Tuck away some time everyday to connect with the One who holds everything in his hands. If this is not a regular practice for you, try starting with just 5 minutes a day. Everyone has 5 minutes to give, make it a habit and see how your relationship with Christ changes.

Chapter 5
Mission

Mission

Well, how about I start with the bad news. God doesn't need you. He doesn't need you for a specific mission. He is an all-powerful, all-knowing, Sovereign King. He doesn't need help getting his mission done. He could snap his fingers and make it happen. He could speak out into nothing, just like he did when he created the world. One of the hardest things in being a disciple of Christ is dealing with this concept. It's really easy to think highly of yourself, and it's easy to start down the mission road with the idea that God needs you to get this mission done and if you don't, it's the end of the world.

But there's good news too.

Even though He doesn't need you to do anything for Him, he invited you to the mission road.

He wants you to join Him in the journey. He thinks you are amazing. He's crazy about you. He sees the whole scope of your life, every tiny detail, and he knows the road map. What looks like a tangled mess surrounding us, actually creates a beautiful mosaic from His perspective. Your experiences, your burdens, the things you love, your relationships, your failures, your visions, and your successes; these all fit together in a way we would never know, unless we saw them from a higher perspective...His perspective.

One of my favorite movies (and another recommendation if you haven't seen it) is the movie *Dead Poets Society*. Robin Williams plays the role of John Keating, a really unconventional teacher in a very traditional all-boys boarding school. These high school boys are going through classes that follow this format (one that you may recognize): get the information, write a paper on it, memorize it, get tested on it. Every class and every year is the same, and it creates the mindset that they must live by the expectations of the culture around them.

John Keating knows that each boy in his classroom will probably make their most life defining decisions over the next ten years; from marriage and children, to career path and financial status. They will put down their roots, and once that happens, it's very hard to make changes. John Keating understands the pressure they are under to meet the expectations of their families and culture, and he wants them to think differently about their lives before it's too late to make changes.

So in one of the most powerful scenes, John Keating jumps onto his desk and begins to walk around on it. He's no longer standing as a professor in front of the class; instead he's towering over the classroom, taking inventory of what's inside.
He asks, "Why do I stand up here? Anybody?"

"To feel taller" someone says.

"No! Thank you for playing Mr. Dalton. I stand upon my desk to remind myself that we must constantly look at things a different way. The world looks very different from up here."

Pausing and staring his class in the eyes, he invites each person to stand on his desk and look at their world from a different perspective. John Keating was trying desperately to convince them to decide their life's pursuit now, not when it's too late.

He continued, "Just when you think you know something, you have to look at it in a different way. Boys, you must strive to find your own voice, and the longer you wait to begin, the less likely you are to find it at all. Thoreau said that 'most men lead lives of quiet desperation'…don't be resigned to that…break out."

You see, most people begin considering a mission later in life, after they've spent years pursuing a lifestyle. They get to the point where they've attained everything they wanted, but still have a growing discontent inside of them. Henry David Thoreau called it "a quiet desperation." So when the dust settles in their lives and their roots have dug in, they begin a searching process. They look at their lives from a higher perspective, and try to find their voice. It's become so common, we call it a mid-life crisis, or quarter-life crisis. Sometimes it happens on key birthdays like 30 or 40. And quite frankly, it's a terrible thing to wait until your roots are in before you stand on the desk in your life. It's terrible because you might find you put roots in where you never wanted them to be. John Keating was trying to get his students to look at their lives from a higher perspective now, so they wouldn't find themselves longing for a different life after its too late.

Mr. Keating was helping his students find their mission. He was asking them to get on a higher level so they could catch a glimpse of their end goal. He wanted his students to see the entirety of their lives and take inventory of their deepest desires, their passions, their dreams, their potential; and use them to find their voice and capture their direction. He was challenging them to not be victims of their destiny, but to be drivers of it. And he knew that if they didn't find it now, if they waited too long, it would be too late.

Your mission is the thing that will guide you through the next several years, and help you put roots down where you will be most satisfied and fulfilled. It's what will be the guiding force in making the major decisions in your life. It will help you navigate the dangerous waters of culture and status quo, so you will never wake up one day wondering how you got there.

The goal of this last chapter is to take inventory of all of the things in your life that you've identified in this book, and to look down the road from a higher perspective at the journey that you've been invited on with Christ. To see if there's any themes or statements that you can hang your hat on in order to guide you through the many decisions that are waiting for you. Simply put, the goal is to identify your mission, or as John Keating put it, "to find your voice."

On A Mission:

I love it when Jesus called the disciples. He didn't make a sales pitch, giving them statistics and resources about what their lives could look like. He didn't wine and dine them to get their buy in. He simply cast out a mission.

Take a look at Matthew 4:18-20:

As Jesus was walking beside the Sea of Galilee, he saw two brothers, Simon called Peter and his brother Andrew. They were casting a net into the lake, for they were fishermen. "Come follow me," Jesus said, "and I will make you fishers of men." At once they left their nets and followed him.

What was the mission? To be fishers of men.

What was the response? At once, they followed.

This simple mission—to be fishers of men—was something that would guide Peter and Andrew through their whole lives. It was something they could hang their hat on at the end of the day and use to help them make the key decisions in their lives. They had opportunities, just like you do. They had a whole culture calling them to be a certain way and to live a certain life, just like you. And they could have let life just happen to them, or they could pursue the mission Jesus was giving them.

Put yourself in their shoes, and consider their thought process:

Should I still fish on the side to make a little extra money?

Should I consider getting married to that girl in town?

Should I keep my boat in storage, just in case?

Is it okay for me to hang out with the hated tax collectors?

Should I avoid the beggars and sick people in the city centers?

Each one of these questions, small and big, could be answered by their mission. Peter and Andrew may not have had a complete view of how everything would turn out in their lives, but they could make decisions along the way that would lead them down the mission road with Jesus. Eventually, they would become the catalysts for moving the gospel across the globe. Peter would become the rock on which the church was built, and their lives would impact generations to come. Even now, 2000 years later, we are studying Peter and Andrew.

This is what a mission does. It helps you in the moving on process by guiding you through one step at a time. It's like lines on a road; at any point you can choose to swerve off, but the lines keep you going in the right direction. Your mission is not something that is far out there, and seemingly unreachable. It is something close that can guide your day to day actions.

My Mission:

All of this can seem very abstract if we don't take a few moments to examine what this looks like in someone's life. So here's an example of how it works in my life. I have a burden for students who don't really know Christ. From the unbeliever to the apathetic, I want them to know Christ and know their kingdom potential. Whenever I watch the news, I can listen to story after story of war, floods, and hurricanes. And while each of these things stir compassion in me, it's very little compared to when I hear the story about the local high school student who was shot, or in a car accident. It makes me want to run to their bedside at the hospital because I am so burdened for students to know what Christ thinks about them.

I am passionate about a lot of things, but I'm probably most passionate about leadership. I am constantly buying books on Amazon about this topic. I am drawn to helping leaders solve problems and navigate obstacles. I love coaching leaders and investing in leaders. I'm an elder at my church, and I'm a leader of a small group. I am passionate about the topic of leadership. Now I'm also passionate about other things too, sports would be one of them. I love watching football and rooting for the Chicago Bears, and I love playing golf and tennis. As soon as the golf courses open in Chicago, I'm there.

I have a vision, simply put, for LeaderTreks. LeaderTreks is the ministry I founded that is focused on developing students into leaders. We run leadership focused mission and wilderness trips, and make resources for youth pastors. We do training for both students and youth workers, all for the purpose of godly leadership development.

When I looked at all of these areas of my life and I considered my gifting and wiring, I was able to formulate a mission statement that was true to where I felt God was leading me. In my life, I want **to develop leaders to fulfill the great commission.** It's a broad statement, but it keeps me directed and focused on the mission road, and more importantly on my journey with Him. Time after time I have come to hard decisions in my life and my mission has helped me stay on track. Here's how it has played out.

Burden

Passion

Vision

Mission

When I was younger, I had a lot to learn about leadership, and a lot of training to go through when it came to leading my own company. So I spent a few years in the business world, learning the ins and outs of organizational leadership. At the same, time I volunteered at a local youth group learning more about student development. Eventually, with enough money saved up, I was able to start my own ministry and really focus on my vision. So now, every day, I am either investing in students or the leaders of students. I want so desperately for people to realize Christ has invited them on the adventure of a lifetime. He has entrusted them with the future of the church and kingdom impact.

I got married a lot later in life. I didn't want to marry someone on a journey that would end up compromising both of our missions; I wanted to be a partner with someone who would make me better as I walked my mission road, and vice versa. I was 46 when I found someone who would be a great partner, and I do not ever regret waiting.

When it came to finding a church, I really had to find a place that not just fit my style, but a place that allowed me to live out my mission and serve in my gifts. I wanted to be in a church where I could help with people development and leadership training.

When it came to buying a house, I needed to make sure it was a place that would accommodate constant hospitality. Developing leaders often means bringing them into your life. And my home has become a regular boarding house for youth workers, people in ministry, and my own staff.

Almost every decision in my life is linked to my mission. I even work out 5 times a week, (often times on the tennis court) so I can be ready for anything God has for me in developing leaders. Some decisions are more clear than others, but by living on a mission, I have been able to find my voice and put long lasting roots down. Had I just gone to college and followed suit, I would have probably made decisions that would hinder me from living out the mission I am on today. I would have put roots down without consulting my future, and I would probably be questioning a lot of things in my life.

Remember Thoreau's words: "many men live lives of quiet desperation." A mission can keep you from that fate.

So What's Your Mission?

For most of you, this is a million dollar question and probably overwhelming. For some of you, it's been clear from the start. No matter what boat you are in, spend some time in the next few pages looking at everything you've identified in this book from a different perspective. Take a step back from the daily grind, and ask yourself hard questions about what the mission road looks like for you.

Take some time to answer the following questions.

My burden is:

I'm passionate about:

My vision is:

My spiritual gifts are:

My unique abilities are:

What are some key words, ideas, or themes that seem related?

Can you see a way these areas intersect or overlap?

Now use your answers to begin writing a mission statement for your life. Remember a mission statement isn't a list, it's simply a statement that keeps you focused. It will guide you through life-altering decisions and keep you on track during hard times.

Chances are, that as you grow, so will your mission. It may morph and develop through experiences and God's revelation. But where it's at now is the starting point for moving on. It's like going on a hike with a map. It's a must-have if you are going to stay safe and ever reach your destination.

If you are unsure about your mission, think of this as wet cement. There's movement in it, adjustments can be made, but it's the first step in paving the way to your destiny.

My Mission Is:

Chapter 6
So Now What?

So Now What?

Jim Elliot is probably one of the most well-known missionaries of all time. He was one of the 5 missionaries who went deep into the jungles of Equador in the 1950's to reach the unreached Waodani tribe. This tribe had been marked by violence, and had already killed several Shell Oil employees in the past. In fact, the tribe was also called the Auca tribe, which is their native word for "savage."

Jim had a mission to reach people for Christ overseas. He wasn't always sure how it would play out, but he felt very strongly about it. With that mission in mind, Jim made decisions that would lead him on his journey with Christ. Jim went to Wheaton College (a private Christian college) to study and lived a little differently than the average college student. He joined the wrestling team right away, knowing that it would keep him physically strong and disciplined (two things that would come in handy on the mission field). While at college Jim also took every opportunity possible to get his feet wet in missions. He stayed with missionaries in Mexico during a summer break. He attended missions conventions and was a member of the Student Foreign Missions Fellowship. Through these experiences and relationships with other missionaries, Jim knew he was being drawn to tribal work in Central America.

When he realized this, began making even more decisions based on his mission, Jim ate different than others. His diet consisted heavily of fruits and vegetables because he knew that would likely be his diet when he served overseas. He decided to study Greek because he figured he would probably be involved with Bible translation if he was going to work with tribes. He even fell in love at Wheaton college, but didn't marry until several years later when he was already in the mission field in Ecuador and felt God's leading.

Jim didn't let any obstacles divert him from his mission. While waiting for one of his friends to join him on the journey to Ecuador, Jim used the several months at home to preach in prisons, teach Sunday school, and hold evangelistic rallies. In the large and in the small, Jim lived on a mission. Whether it was his diet, his friends, his free time, or what classes he took, Jim lived on a mission.

In one of Jim's journal entries in 1949, he wrote *"He is no fool who gives what he cannot keep, to gain that which he cannot lose."*[1]

This quote in many ways describes Jim's life. He was willing to give up so many things that were off mission, and he held unswervingly to Christ on the mission road, even when confronted with death. Sadly, at the age of 29, Jim and his four teammates were speared to death by the members of the Waodani tribe that they had gone to reach. It was a tragic event that rocked the world. Even Time Magazine did a 10-page spread on it. But it also inspired Jim's wife and others to go on with the mission and eventually see many of the Waodani become Christ followers.

Mission Requires Action

I love the story of Jim's life because it so clearly paints what life on a mission looks like. Jim didn't wait to arrive somewhere, or graduate college to start living on a mission. No one wakes up one day and does an Iron Man Triathlon; they make small decisions and sacrifices that train them for the big day. In the same way, our mission will not be accomplished some day way out in the future unless we begin making mission-minded decisions now in our lives.

Mission requires action, and it requires it now.

God has called you to your mission. He invited you. You now have the responsibility to accomplish it. He decided before time that this would be the heartbeat of your life, and he wants you to join him.

Here are some questions to help guide you through the actions you can take now, in order to "move on" in a way that takes hold of your mission.

What are some resources you need to accomplish your mission? (things, experiences, relationships)

What information do you need to start? What do you need to learn?

What changes do you need to make in your life in order to pursue God's mission now?

Do you need to get advice or wisdom from anyone in your life? Do you need someone to keep you accountable?

Remember back to the beginning of this book, when Crystal packed her bag and went to college? She did it with the mindset that "whatever happens, happens." This cost her. She missed a lot of opportunities to pursue God and pursue His unique plan for her, because she waited for the day when she would "arrive." The day when a diploma would be framed above her desk, and she was ready to say, "what should I do with my life?" By the time that day would come, she would already be locked into habits and a lifestyle that could prevent her from new dreams.

God didn't create us to dress in Sunday clothes and sit in church pews. He didn't intend for us to live boring lives that followed suit and followed rules. He made us for something great. He mapped out an adventure for us that will cause the adrenaline to pump through our veins and our eyes to widen. He has called you to something great. He has invited you to be His solution in this broken world. And there is no way it can be done by living in the status quo. He has called you to more than that.

Will you accept the invitation?

Appendix

Passion Survey

On the following pages you will find a list of many different things a person could be deeply passionate about in life. They range from hobbies to careers to communities. It's important to note the rating scale under each individual example. As you read each example, fill in the corresponding bubble based on your gut reaction. While you may thoroughly enjoy watching sports, a deep passion for the game may not well up inside you. At the same time, you may wish for a deep community, yet that desire does not take form in your life on a regular basis. The things you are deeply passionate about are the things that consume your thoughts. If you know an area of passion in your life that is not represented here, add it in one of the blank spots at the end.

Administration

Not Interested	Interested	Engaging	Somewhat Passionate	Highly Passionate
①	②	③	④	⑤

Adult Ministries

Not Interested	Interested	Engaging	Somewhat Passionate	Highly Passionate
①	②	③	④	⑤

Agriculture/Farming

Not Interested	Interested	Engaging	Somewhat Passionate	Highly Passionate
①	②	③	④	⑤

Antiques and Collectibles

Not Interested	Interested	Engaging	Somewhat Passionate	Highly Passionate
①	②	③	④	⑤

Architecture

Not Interested	Interested	Engaging	Somewhat Passionate	Highly Passionate
①	②	③	④	⑤

Art

Not Interested	Interested	Engaging	Somewhat Passionate	Highly Passionate
1	2	3	4	5

Athletics

Not Interested	Interested	Engaging	Somewhat Passionate	Highly Passionate
1	2	3	4	5

Automobiles

Not Interested	Interested	Engaging	Somewhat Passionate	Highly Passionate
1	2	3	4	5

Board Games

Not Interested	Interested	Engaging	Somewhat Passionate	Highly Passionate
1	2	3	4	5

Business

Not Interested	Interested	Engaging	Somewhat Passionate	Highly Passionate
1	2	3	4	5

Camping

Not Interested	Interested	Engaging	Somewhat Passionate	Highly Passionate
1	2	3	4	5

Caring for People

Not Interested	Interested	Engaging	Somewhat Passionate	Highly Passionate
1	2	3	4	5

Carpentry

Not Interested	Interested	Engaging	Somewhat Passionate	Highly Passionate
1	2	3	4	5

Children's Ministry

Not Interested	Interested	Engaging	Somewhat Passionate	Highly Passionate
1	2	3	4	5

Clean Water

Not Interested	Interested	Engaging	Somewhat Passionate	Highly Passionate
1	2	3	4	5

Comics

Not Interested	Interested	Engaging	Somewhat Passionate	Highly Passionate
1	2	3	4	5

Community

Not Interested	Interested	Engaging	Somewhat Passionate	Highly Passionate
1	2	3	4	5

Computer Technology

Not Interested	Interested	Engaging	Somewhat Passionate	Highly Passionate
1	2	3	4	5

Cooking/Food

Not Interested	Interested	Engaging	Somewhat Passionate	Highly Passionate
1	2	3	4	5

Counseling Others

Not Interested	Interested	Engaging	Somewhat Passionate	Highly Passionate
1	2	3	4	5

Craft Making

Not Interested	Interested	Engaging	Somewhat Passionate	Highly Passionate
1	2	3	4	5

Current Events

Not Interested	Interested	Engaging	Somewhat Passionate	Highly Passionate
1	2	3	4	5

Dance

Not Interested	Interested	Engaging	Somewhat Passionate	Highly Passionate
1	2	3	4	5

Debate

Not Interested	Interested	Engaging	Somewhat Passionate	Highly Passionate
①	②	③	④	⑤

Different Cultures

Not Interested	Interested	Engaging	Somewhat Passionate	Highly Passionate
①	②	③	④	⑤

Discipleship

Not Interested	Interested	Engaging	Somewhat Passionate	Highly Passionate
①	②	③	④	⑤

Education

Not Interested	Interested	Engaging	Somewhat Passionate	Highly Passionate
①	②	③	④	⑤

Encouraging Others

Not Interested	Interested	Engaging	Somewhat Passionate	Highly Passionate
①	②	③	④	⑤

Ending Abuse

Not Interested	Interested	Engaging	Somewhat Passionate	Highly Passionate
①	②	③	④	⑤

Engineering

Not Interested	Interested	Engaging	Somewhat Passionate	Highly Passionate
①	②	③	④	⑤

Evangelism/Outreach

Not Interested	Interested	Engaging	Somewhat Passionate	Highly Passionate
①	②	③	④	⑤

Faith

Not Interested	Interested	Engaging	Somewhat Passionate	Highly Passionate
①	②	③	④	⑤

Family

Not Interested	Interested	Engaging	Somewhat Passionate	Highly Passionate
1	2	3	4	5

Fashion

Not Interested	Interested	Engaging	Somewhat Passionate	Highly Passionate
1	2	3	4	5

Fighting Diseases

Not Interested	Interested	Engaging	Somewhat Passionate	Highly Passionate
1	2	3	4	5

Finance

Not Interested	Interested	Engaging	Somewhat Passionate	Highly Passionate
1	2	3	4	5

Fostering Relationships

Not Interested	Interested	Engaging	Somewhat Passionate	Highly Passionate
1	2	3	4	5

Giving

Not Interested	Interested	Engaging	Somewhat Passionate	Highly Passionate
1	2	3	4	5

Graphic Design

Not Interested	Interested	Engaging	Somewhat Passionate	Highly Passionate
1	2	3	4	5

Health and Fitness

Not Interested	Interested	Engaging	Somewhat Passionate	Highly Passionate
1	2	3	4	5

Health Care

Not Interested	Interested	Engaging	Somewhat Passionate	Highly Passionate
1	2	3	4	5

History

Not Interested	Interested	Engaging	Somewhat Passionate	Highly Passionate
1	2	3	4	5

Home and Gardening

Not Interested	Interested	Engaging	Somewhat Passionate	Highly Passionate
1	2	3	4	5

Hospitality

Not Interested	Interested	Engaging	Somewhat Passionate	Highly Passionate
1	2	3	4	5

Human Rights

Not Interested	Interested	Engaging	Somewhat Passionate	Highly Passionate
1	2	3	4	5

Hunting and Fishing

Not Interested	Interested	Engaging	Somewhat Passionate	Highly Passionate
1	2	3	4	5

Interior Design

Not Interested	Interested	Engaging	Somewhat Passionate	Highly Passionate
1	2	3	4	5

Journalism

Not Interested	Interested	Engaging	Somewhat Passionate	Highly Passionate
1	2	3	4	5

Justice

Not Interested	Interested	Engaging	Somewhat Passionate	Highly Passionate
1	2	3	4	5

Languages

Not Interested	Interested	Engaging	Somewhat Passionate	Highly Passionate
1	2	3	4	5

Law/Political Science

Not Interested	Interested	Engaging	Somewhat Passionate	Highly Passionate
1	2	3	4	5

Leadership

Not Interested	Interested	Engaging	Somewhat Passionate	Highly Passionate
1	2	3	4	5

Music

Not Interested	Interested	Engaging	Somewhat Passionate	Highly Passionate
1	2	3	4	5

Literature

Not Interested	Interested	Engaging	Somewhat Passionate	Highly Passionate
1	2	3	4	5

Management

Not Interested	Interested	Engaging	Somewhat Passionate	Highly Passionate
1	2	3	4	5

Mathematics

Not Interested	Interested	Engaging	Somewhat Passionate	Highly Passionate
1	2	3	4	5

Meditation

Not Interested	Interested	Engaging	Somewhat Passionate	Highly Passionate
1	2	3	4	5

Mentoring

Not Interested	Interested	Engaging	Somewhat Passionate	Highly Passionate
1	2	3	4	5

Missions

Not Interested	Interested	Engaging	Somewhat Passionate	Highly Passionate
1	2	3	4	5

Movies and Film

Not Interested	Interested	Engaging	Somewhat Passionate	Highly Passionate
1	2	3	4	5

Pets

Not Interested	Interested	Engaging	Somewhat Passionate	Highly Passionate
1	2	3	4	5

Philosophy

Not Interested	Interested	Engaging	Somewhat Passionate	Highly Passionate
1	2	3	4	5

Photography

Not Interested	Interested	Engaging	Somewhat Passionate	Highly Passionate
1	2	3	4	5

Playing Music

Not Interested	Interested	Engaging	Somewhat Passionate	Highly Passionate
1	2	3	4	5

Politics

Not Interested	Interested	Engaging	Somewhat Passionate	Highly Passionate
1	2	3	4	5

Poverty

Not Interested	Interested	Engaging	Somewhat Passionate	Highly Passionate
1	2	3	4	5

Prayer

Not Interested	Interested	Engaging	Somewhat Passionate	Highly Passionate
1	2	3	4	5

Pro-Life Issues

Not Interested	Interested	Engaging	Somewhat Passionate	Highly Passionate
1	2	3	4	5

Protecting the Environment

Not Interested	Interested	Engaging	Somewhat Passionate	Highly Passionate
1	2	3	4	5

Public Speaking

Not Interested	Interested	Engaging	Somewhat Passionate	Highly Passionate
1	2	3	4	5

Reading

Not Interested	Interested	Engaging	Somewhat Passionate	Highly Passionate
1	2	3	4	5

Rehabilitation Work

Not Interested	Interested	Engaging	Somewhat Passionate	Highly Passionate
1	2	3	4	5

Sciences

Not Interested	Interested	Engaging	Somewhat Passionate	Highly Passionate
1	2	3	4	5

Self Discovery

Not Interested	Interested	Engaging	Somewhat Passionate	Highly Passionate
1	2	3	4	5

Service

Not Interested	Interested	Engaging	Somewhat Passionate	Highly Passionate
1	2	3	4	5

Sewing/Knitting

Not Interested	Interested	Engaging	Somewhat Passionate	Highly Passionate
1	2	3	4	5

Small Groups

Not Interested	Interested	Engaging	Somewhat Passionate	Highly Passionate
1	2	3	4	5

Social Services

Not Interested	Interested	Engaging	Somewhat Passionate	Highly Passionate
①	②	③	④	⑤

Spending Time in the Outdoors

Not Interested	Interested	Engaging	Somewhat Passionate	Highly Passionate
①	②	③	④	⑤

Sports

Not Interested	Interested	Engaging	Somewhat Passionate	Highly Passionate
①	②	③	④	⑤

Student Leadership

Not Interested	Interested	Engaging	Somewhat Passionate	Highly Passionate
①	②	③	④	⑤

Studying the Bible

Not Interested	Interested	Engaging	Somewhat Passionate	Highly Passionate
①	②	③	④	⑤

Teaching Others

Not Interested	Interested	Engaging	Somewhat Passionate	Highly Passionate
①	②	③	④	⑤

Television

Not Interested	Interested	Engaging	Somewhat Passionate	Highly Passionate
①	②	③	④	⑤

Theater

Not Interested	Interested	Engaging	Somewhat Passionate	Highly Passionate
①	②	③	④	⑤

Theology

Not Interested	Interested	Engaging	Somewhat Passionate	Highly Passionate
①	②	③	④	⑤

Training Animals

Not Interested	Interested	Engaging	Somewhat Passionate	Highly Passionate
1	2	3	4	5

Travel

Not Interested	Interested	Engaging	Somewhat Passionate	Highly Passionate
1	2	3	4	5

Video Games

Not Interested	Interested	Engaging	Somewhat Passionate	Highly Passionate
1	2	3	4	5

Wildlife

Not Interested	Interested	Engaging	Somewhat Passionate	Highly Passionate
1	2	3	4	5

Worship

Not Interested	Interested	Engaging	Somewhat Passionate	Highly Passionate
1	2	3	4	5

Writing

Not Interested	Interested	Engaging	Somewhat Passionate	Highly Passionate
1	2	3	4	5

Youth Ministry

Not Interested	Interested	Engaging	Somewhat Passionate	Highly Passionate
1	2	3	4	5

Create Your Own: _____

Not Interested	Interested	Engaging	Somewhat Passionate	Highly Passionate
1	2	3	4	5

Create Your Own: _____

Not Interested	Interested	Engaging	Somewhat Passionate	Highly Passionate
1	2	3	4	5

Create Your Own: _____

Not Interested	Interested	Engaging	Somewhat Passionate	Highly Passionate
(1)	(2)	(3)	(4)	(5)

Create Your Own: _____

Not Interested	Interested	Engaging	Somewhat Passionate	Highly Passionate
(1)	(2)	(3)	(4)	(5)

Create Your Own: _____

Not Interested	Interested	Engaging	Somewhat Passionate	Highly Passionate
(1)	(2)	(3)	(4)	(5)

Now that you've gone through the list, take a look at your answers, as well as your answers to the questions on page 24. Write down what you think are the 3 things you are most passionate about and use the space provided to explain in your own words why these things are important to you and how these passions play out in your life.

Make sure to really think deeply about why you are passionate about something, because passions can sometimes disguise themselves. Someone that seems to be really passionate about sports may actually be passionate about strategy or teambuilding. It may just manifest itself in sports.

Unique Abilities Profile

If you are like most people, you've probably learned that you do a few things especially well. These are abilities that come naturally for you. What makes these abilities important is they are transferable—you can use them in a wide range of situations. You will also find yourself drawn to situations where you can use these abilities and enjoy doing so when you have the opportunity. This profile will help you to identify your unique God-given abilities.

Each person's unique set of abilities emerges over a long period of time and is reinforced through in a variety of situations. Your unique abilities do not change over time. But as you mature new abilities may show themselves for the first time.

Depending on how aware you are of the things you do well, you may already have identified one or more abilities as unique personal strengths. Still, you can gain a deeper understanding of your unique abilities and even identify previously hidden abilities by analyzing your positive experiences.

One caution: some people find this difficult to do. If you have difficulty identifying abilities in the profile, ask an adult to work through it with you.

Start by identifying a number of positive experiences where you:
- were naturally interested in getting involved
- were an active participant
- felt a sense of enjoyment or satisfaction

Here are some simple steps to identify and analyze your positive experiences:

1. Think back over the past few years of your life. Make a list of as many positive experiences as you can recall, and list them below :

2. Next, go back and circle the 5 experiences that stand out as the most satisfying to you, regardless of whether anyone else thought they were important. Transfer your list of experiences to the spaces below, and jot down a few notes about the main things you did as part of each experience. Simply summarize what you did and how you did it…

3. Next, number your experiences 1-5 and compare each one to this list of abilities. Starting with the first experience, remember what you did and how you did it. Then place a check in the box for any abilities that you used in that experience. When you get to the bottom of the list, do the same for the rest of the experiences. This is not an exhaustive list of abilities but satisfactorily covers the major areas.

	Experience 1	Experience 2	Experience 3	Experience 4	Experience 5
Accepting challenges/taking risks					
Analyzing					
Assembling/installing					
Assisting/helping					
Befriending/encouraging/affirming					
Being adaptable					
Building relationships					
Building/crafting					
Coaching/mentoring					
Comforting/caring for others					
Consulting/advising					
Cooperating/collaborating					
Coordinating/delegating					
Counseling					
Creative thinking					
Critical thinking					
Decision-making					
Designing/creating					
Directing/taking charge					
Finding/acquiring resources					
Improving processes/methods					
Innovating/inventing					
Inspiring/motivating					
Leading discussions					
Learning					
Listening/being sensitive					
Managing/organizing information					
Mediating/resolving conflict					

	Experience 1	Experience 2	Experience 3	Experience 4	Experience 5
Monitoring/correcting					
Negotiating/bargaining					
Operating/repairing/maintaining equipment					
Organizing					
Overseeing					
Performing/entertaining					
Pioneering/initiating change					
Planning					
Problem-solving					
Producing/following-through					
Public speaking					
Recruiting					
Selling/promoting/persuading					
Setting/meeting deadlines					
Showing appreciation/recognizing					
Strategizing					
Studying/researching					
Summarizing/reporting information					
Supervising					
Teaching/training					
Using technology effectively					
Working independently					
Working with my hands					
Writing/editing					

4. Once you have completed your analysis for all 5 experiences, review the checkmarks you made. Circle any abilities with more than one checkmark. This means you used this ability in multiple experiences. Now look at your list of circled items and identify 5 to 7 abilities that you believe are your unique set of abilities. List them below.

A Final Word

Again, remember that many people find it difficult to identify their own strengths, particularly in terms of abilities. For most of us, our strengths are too close for us to see them clearly. Don't become discouraged if this is difficult for you to do. We also tend to discount what we do well, especially if a particular activity comes easily for us. We assume that if it's easy for us then it's probably easy for other people too. Be assured that this is not true. The abilities that are easiest for us are often that way because these are special abilities or strengths that are gifts from God. We also tend to use them more often and benefit from that regular practice.

Now that you know what to look for, take time to review new positive experiences from time to time. Doing so will help you refine your understanding of—and your ability to apply—your unique God-given abilities.

Spiritual Gifts Assessment

Welcome to an exciting opportunity.

For many of you, this will be your first chance to identify your unique pattern of spiritual gifts. These are the special God-given abilities that are a key component of your "divine design."

Your awareness of your gifts will grow over time as you mature spiritually and as you receive affirmation from others. Your level of assurance will grow through your experience of using your gifts effectively and becoming comfortable with who you are at your best.

This profile is designed to help you identify your spiritual gifts. As with any such profile, your results will only be as accurate as the answers you give. Be sure to answer based on who you really are, not who you would like to be or who others think you ought to be.

Read the following statements carefully. Enter your ratings on the response sheet based on how well the statement describes you, using the following scale:

(**5**) Definitely Me

(**4**) Very Much Like Me

(**3**) Somewhat Like Me

(**2**) Not Much Like Me

(**1**) Definitely Not Me

1.	I regularly encourage others to trust God, even when circumstances seem bleak.	5	4	3	2	1
2.	Others see me as caring and sensitive, and open up to me about their feelings.	5	4	3	2	1
3.	I willingly accept responsibility for leading groups that lack direction or motivation.	5	4	3	2	1
4.	I feel compelled to tell others about the inconsistencies I see and their impact.	5	4	3	2	1
5.	I seem better able than most people to sense when others are in need of a lift.	5	4	3	2	1
6.	I find it easy to engage non-believers in conversations about spiritual matters.	5	4	3	2	1
7.	I feel like a partner with the people and organizations I support financially.	5	4	3	2	1
8.	Others often ask me to research topics they want to understand more fully.	5	4	3	2	1
9.	I enjoy guiding and supporting individuals and groups seeking to learn and grow.	5	4	3	2	1
10.	Others see me as highly organized and look for my help in managing projects.	5	4	3	2	1
11.	I find that I am more adventurous and willing to take risks than most people.	5	4	3	2	1
12.	I enjoy analyzing difficult problems and discovering simple, practical solutions.	5	4	3	2	1
13.	I often seem to see matters of injustice or unfairness more clearly than other people.	5	4	3	2	1
14.	I enjoy working unrecognized behind the scenes to support the work of others.	5	4	3	2	1
15.	When I teach, I communicate clearly, and find it easy to engage people in learning.	5	4	3	2	1

		Definitely me	Very much like me	Somewhat like me	Not much like me	Definitely not me
16.	I am confident that God helps us to do great things when we trust Him.	5	4	3	2	1
17.	I am easily moved by others' experience of heartache or suffering.	5	4	3	2	1
18.	I adjust my leadership style to work well with a variety of individuals or groups.	5	4	3	2	1
19.	I seem better able than most people to see the truth of what is really going on.	5	4	3	2	1
20.	Others see me as a positive, optimistic person who can make others feel good.	5	4	3	2	1
21.	I seem to be more concerned than most to share the gospel with non-believers.	5	4	3	2	1
22.	I feel deep satisfaction knowing my giving is making a real difference.	5	4	3	2	1
23.	I enjoy becoming more of an expert on a topic, and sharing my knowledge with others.	5	4	3	2	1
24.	I am more willing than other people to invest time in helping others grow as believers.	5	4	3	2	1
25.	I enjoy being relied upon to organize people and tasks to meet a goal.	5	4	3	2	1
26.	Others see me as a change agent and look to me to lead new undertakings.	5	4	3	2	1
27.	I frequently am able to see potential solutions to problems that others cannot.	5	4	3	2	1
28.	Others see me as a person of strong convictions and willing to speak out.	5	4	3	2	1
29.	I find fulfillment in faithfully performing tasks others see as unglamorous.	5	4	3	2	1
30.	I am confident in my ability to help others learn and apply knowledge and skills.	5	4	3	2	1

		Definitely me	Very much like me	Somewhat like me	Not much like me	Definitely not me
31.	I think I am more confident than most in trusting God, even in the hard times.	5	4	3	2	1
32.	I enjoy helping people that others may regard as undeserving or beyond help.	5	4	3	2	1
33.	I can successfully motivate, guide, and manage others to reach important goals.	5	4	3	2	1
34.	Others see me as insightful, a good judge of people and situations.	5	4	3	2	1
35.	People often seek me out when they are looking for affirmation or encouragement.	5	4	3	2	1
36.	Others see me as being confident in my faith, and ready and willing to share it.	5	4	3	2	1
37.	I give more generously than most people to church and other worthwhile causes.	5	4	3	2	1
38.	I share what I know confidently and clearly, helping others to understand.	5	4	3	2	1
39.	Others see me as a patient, supportive person who brings out the best in others.	5	4	3	2	1
40.	I am skilled at planning, organizing, and managing even complex projects.	5	4	3	2	1
41.	I am always looking for new experiences and love bringing about change.	5	4	3	2	1
42.	When asked to help solve a problem, people usually end up taking my advice.	5	4	3	2	1
43.	I feel a strong sense of responsibility to take a stand for what is right and true.	5	4	3	2	1
44.	I can see how my support with the little things helps others accomplish more.	5	4	3	2	1
45.	I believe I am more motivated to want to help others learn than most people.	5	4	3	2	1

		Definitely me	Very much like me	Somewhat like me	Not much like me	Definitely not me
46.	Others see me as having strong faith, able to provide spiritual encouragement.	5	4	3	2	1
47.	It makes me happy to bring comfort, hope, and joy to people facing difficulties.	5	4	3	2	1
48.	I seem better able than most to help a group work together to achieve its goals.	5	4	3	2	1
49.	I always look below the surface to try to see the truth about people and situations.	5	4	3	2	1
50.	I am drawn to people who are confused or troubled, and try to cheer them up.	5	4	3	2	1
51.	In my relationships with non-believers, I regularly find ways to share my faith.	5	4	3	2	1
52.	It is important to manage my finances well so I can support causes I believe in.	5	4	3	2	1
53.	I like sharing knowledge that improves others' understanding and effectiveness.	5	4	3	2	1
54.	I willingly help others to grow in their faith and to improve their Christian walk.	5	4	3	2	1
55.	I enjoy helping a group to work efficiently and effectively to complete a project.	5	4	3	2	1
56.	I enjoy the challenge of trying new things, despite the unknowns or risks involved.	5	4	3	2	1
57.	I seem to see practical solutions to problems more readily than others.	5	4	3	2	1
58.	I am willing to speak out on matters of right and wrong even if unpopular.	5	4	3	2	1
59.	I seem more willing than most to pitch in wherever I can without being asked.	5	4	3	2	1
60.	Others see me as someone who can make difficult concepts easier to learn.	5	4	3	2	1

61.	I find it natural and easy to trust God to answer prayer for myself and others.	5	4	3	2	1
62.	I seem more compassionate than most, especially with people who are hurting.	5	4	3	2	1
63.	Others naturally look to me to lead, especially when facing big challenges.	5	4	3	2	1
64.	I can see through phoniness, deception, or error, usually before others are able to.	5	4	3	2	1
65.	I challenge people to look for and affirm the good in themselves and others.	5	4	3	2	1
66.	I like people to know I am a Christian and want them to ask me about my faith.	5	4	3	2	1
67.	I willingly contribute to projects needing my support or people in financial need.	5	4	3	2	1
68.	I think I am better than most people at gathering and sharing information.	5	4	3	2	1
69.	I see the things that hold people back and find ways to help them overcome.	5	4	3	2	1
70.	I think I am more organized than most, better able to manage complex tasks.	5	4	3	2	1
71.	My ability to adapt to new situations makes me comfortable with change.	5	4	3	2	1
72.	Others see me as having a lot of common sense and ask me for advice.	5	4	3	2	1
73.	I am comfortable challenging others to change their thoughts and actions.	5	4	3	2	1
74.	Others see me as always willing to pitch in and do even the smallest routine tasks.	5	4	3	2	1
75.	I enjoy preparing to teach - organizing and planning interesting learning experiences.	5	4	3	2	1

Scoring Guide

Response Sheet

Enter your responses in the appropriate boxes below. Place your score for question #1 in the box marked #1, and so on. After transferring all of your scores, add up the scores for each row and place the total in the column on the right.

					Totals
1.	16.	31.	46.	61.	**1.**
2.	17.	32.	47.	62.	**2.**
3.	18.	33.	48.	63.	**3.**
4.	19.	34.	49.	64.	**4.**
5.	20.	35.	50.	65.	**5.**
6.	21.	36.	51.	66.	**6.**
7.	22.	37.	52.	67.	**7.**
8.	23.	38.	53.	68.	**8.**
9.	24.	39.	54.	69.	**9.**
10.	25.	40.	55.	70.	**10.**
11.	26.	41.	56.	71.	**11.**
12.	27.	42.	57.	72.	**12.**
13.	28.	43.	58.	73.	**13.**
14.	29.	44.	59.	74.	**14.**
15.	30.	45.	60.	75.	**15.**

Enter your totals from the *Response Sheet* in the appropriate spaces below.

	Gift	Description
1.	**Believing** (*Faith*)	Believing is a special God-given ability to trust God's will and act on it with an unwavering belief in God's concern, presence, and active participation.
2.	**Comforting** (*Mercy*)	Comforting is a special God-given ability to understand and come alongside people who are troubled or suffering, bringing them comfort, insight, and hope.
3.	**Directing** (*Leadership*)	Directing is a special God-given ability to instill vision, motivate, and guide people to work together effectively to achieve worthwhile goals.
4.	**Discerning** (*Discernment*)	Discerning is a special God-given ability to distinguish between truth and error, good and evil, and to show good judgment in matters involving character and relationships.
5.	**Encouraging** (*Exhortation*)	Encouraging is a special God-given ability to affirm, uplift, and restore confidence to individuals who are feeling discouraged or defeated.
6.	**Evangelizing** (*Evangelism*)	Evangelizing is a special God-given ability to effectively communicate the Good News of Jesus Christ to non-believers so they can respond and begin to grow in their faith.
7.	**Giving** (*Contributing*)	Giving is a special God-given ability to contribute cheerfully, generously, and regularly to the church and other important ministries, causes, and people in need.
8.	**Learning** (*Knowledge*)	Learning is a special God-given ability to gather, analyze, and share information appropriately with others, leading to greater understanding and insight.
9.	**Mentoring** (*Pastor/Shepherding*)	Mentoring is a special God-given ability to guide and support individuals or groups as they grow in their faith and in their capacity for ministry.
10.	**Organizing** (*Administration*)	Organizing is a special God-given ability to plan, organize tasks, and follow through so that complex projects are completed efficiently and effectively.
11.	**Pioneering** (*Apostleship*)	Pioneering is a special God-given ability to launch new ventures or lead change, confidently moving forward despite uncertainty or risk.
12.	**Problem-Solving** (*Wisdom*)	Problem-solving is a special God-given ability to provide practical advice that leads to timely, effective resolution of problems.

13.	**Speaking Out** *(Prophet)*	Speaking Out is a special God-given ability to declare God's truth boldly and publicly for the purpose of correction or instruction.
14.	**Supporting** *(Helps)*	Supporting is a special God-given ability to provide practical, behind-the-scenes help that frees others to accomplish more than they might otherwise be capable of achieving.
15.	**Teaching** *(Teacher)*	Teaching is a special God-given ability to organize and clearly communicate knowledge and skills to others, and to motivate them to master and apply what they are learning.

Review your scores and identify the 2 or 3 spiritual gifts that appear to be your strongest (higher score being stronger) and list these below.

My spiritual gifts may possibly include:

_____

_____

_____

Next, take some time to learn more about these gifts. For each of your strongest gifts, review the gift summaries on the following pages. Take time to understand what each gift is and the unique contribution it enables you to make when you use it wisely. Think of examples where you have been able to use each gift effectively. How did it feel? What results did you achieve? Have you ever experienced any of the problems described in the Potential Pitfalls section of the summary?

Believing (Faith)

Basic Definition
Believing is a special God-given ability to trust God's will and act on it, with an unwavering belief in God's concern, presence, and active participation.

Unique Leadership Contribution
People with this gift trust God to answer prayer and encourage others to do so, confident in God's help, even in difficult times or in the face of opposition.

This Gift in Scripture
This gift is listed in 1 Corinthians 12:9 where it is usually translated as "faith" or "special faith."

This Gift in Use
People with this gift keep moving forward with confidence, undaunted by obstacles, encouraged by a deeply-rooted belief in God's unending faithfulness and constant care. They are also often the true prayer warriors of the church, lifting its needs to the Lord and seeking His will. When this gift is absent in the church, people can come to doubt God's goodness or His love and concern for His people.

This Gift in a Team
When the going gets tough, people with this gift step up and encourage the rest of the team to keep moving forward, trusting God for strength, guidance, and success.

Typical Strengths
People with this gift tend to be confident, optimistic, prayerful, and reliant on God. By declaring their own trust in God, they encourage others to move forward in faith too.

Potential Pitfalls
People with this gift can become weary and discouraged - or even angry and critical - when others do not share their confidence in God's concern or participation. Using this gift wisely involves remembering and reminding others of the many examples of God's faithfulness in the past, even during the bleakest times.

Comforting (Mercy)

Basic Definition
Comforting is a special God-given ability to understand and come alongside people who are troubled or suffering, bringing them comfort, insight, and hope.

Unique Leadership Contribution
People with this gift patiently and compassionately help hurting people deal with painful experiences, even those whom others feel are undeserving or beyond help.

This Gift in Scripture
This gift is listed in Romans 12:8 where it is usually translated as "showing mercy" or "showing kindness."

This Gift in Use
People with this gift have a unique capacity for providing timely, practical support to hurting people, seemingly with endless patience, compassion, and joy in their hearts. They respond caringly to others' deepest needs, yet are able to look past their problems and circumstances and see their true worth as if through the eyes of God. When this gift is absent in the church, those who are truly needy will receive too little attention.

This Gift in a Team
In the life of any team there will be times when people need, more than anything, to be comforted by someone who comes alongside even as others pull back.

Typical Strengths
People with this gift tend to be caring, sensitive, and tolerant—natural burden bearers. They sense when people are down, and find ways to be there for them.

Potential Pitfalls
Sometimes, people with this gift become weighed down from carrying the burdens of others. Another problem may be that they may unintentionally enable others to avoid facing their difficulties or making hard choices. Using this gift wisely involves helping hurting people to deal with the underlying causes of their problems and not covering them up.

Directing (leadership)

Basic Definition

Directing is a special God-given ability to instill vision, motivate, and guide people to work together effectively to achieve worthwhile goals.

Unique Leadership Contribution

People with this gift willingly take responsibility for directing groups, managing people, and resources effectively, and challenging others to perform at the highest level.

This Gift in Scripture

This gift is listed in Romans 12:8 where it is usually translated as "leadership" or "he who leads."

This Gift in Use

People with this gift help others aspire to and achieve lofty goals. They understand the importance of getting people to perform at their best, both individually and as a group. They relish the opportunity to be in a position of leadership where they can influence the performance of a group that is doing meaningful work. When this gift is absent in the church, people will find themselves falling well short of their potential.

This Gift in a Team

People with this gift are the natural leaders that all teams need to ensure that their efforts are guided by a vision worth pursuing and strategies worth implementing.

Typical Strengths

People with this gift tend to be goal-oriented, decisive, inspiring, and persuasive. They will tend to rise to the top in most groups, emerging naturally as the leader.

Potential Pitfalls

People with this gift need to avoid being over-confident in their own abilities and possibly pushing others away by their perceived arrogance or forcefulness. They can also get stuck in their own ways of doing things, becoming intolerant of others. Using this gift wisely involves building credibility, mutual trust, and support with followers.

Discerning *(Discernment)*

Basic Definition

Discerning is a special God-given ability to distinguish between truth and error, good and evil, and to show good judgment in matters involving character and relationships.

Unique Leadership Contribution

People with this gift reliably distinguish between truth and error, good and evil, readily seeing through phoniness and deceit to perceive what is really going on.

This Gift in Scripture

This gift is listed in 1 Corinthians 12:10 where it is usually translated as "distinguishing between spirits" or "discerning of spirits."

This Gift in Use

People with this gift are unusually capable of recognizing inconsistencies in relationships, behavior, motives, teaching, and everyday practices. They quickly perceive the truth about these things, understand the potential consequences, and warn others to be on guard in order to avoid potentially risky situations. When this gift is absent in the church, people fall prey to false teaching or misguided leadership.

This Gift in a Team

At times, a team will find itself in situations where things are not really as they appear and must rely on the finely-tuned perception of someone with this gift to see the truth.

Typical Strengths

People with this gift are insightful, intuitive, and objective. They will often see things differently than others and will strongly defend their views if challenged.

Potential Pitfalls

People with this gift may need to work hard to avoid being seen by others as harsh and inflexible when sharing their insights, especially when their perceptions run counter to what others are thinking. Using this gift wisely involves taking the time to hear others' opinions, and to seek and share evidence that confirms what they think they are seeing.

Encouraging (Exhortation)

Basic Definition
Encouraging is a special God-given ability to affirm, uplift, and restore confidence to individuals who are feeling discouraged or defeated.

Unique Leadership Contribution
People with this gift sense the needs of others, particularly when they are feeling down, and provide much-appreciated reassurance and cheering up so they can carry on.

This Gift in Scripture
This gift is listed in Romans 12:8 where it is usually translated as "encouraging" or "exhortation."

This Gift in Use
People with this gift readily tune in to others who are in need of a boost. Typically positive and enthusiastic, they sense how others feel and what they need to do to encourage them. Sometimes they challenge or confront, and at other times they cheer up, applaud, or affirm. Whatever the situation, their goal is to help others feel better about themselves. When this gift is absent from a church, people can feel overwhelmed and give up.

This Gift in a Team
Every team needs at least one dedicated cheerleader, and that's a role people with this gift relish. When the going gets tough, they help people stay up and keep moving toward the goal.

Typical Strengths
People with this gift are usually sensitive, positive, and enthusiastic. They see the good in every person, the possibilities in every problem, and the light at the end of the tunnel.

Potential Pitfalls
At times, people with this gift can come across as too simplistic or idealistic. Others don't always appreciate their sunny disposition and unwavering optimism. Using this gift wisely involves acknowledging the reality of the circumstances people are facing and finding ways to offer not only encouragement, but also concrete, practical help.

Evangelizing *(Evangelism)*

Basic Definition

Evangelizing is a special God-given ability to effectively communicate the Good News of Jesus Christ to non-believers so they can respond and begin to grow in their faith.

Unique Leadership Contribution

People with this gift find opportunities to build relationships with non-believers, comfortably sharing their faith, and inviting people to decide to follow Christ.

This Gift in Scripture

This gift is listed in Ephesians 4:11 where it is usually translated as "evangelists."

This Gift in Use

People with this gift communicate the Gospel with ease and effectiveness. They seek opportunities to build relationships with non-believers in order to demonstrate the good news of God's love in practical ways, and to get to know people better. This allows them to share their faith in ways that speak directly to the deepest needs of others. When this gift is absent from a church, people are reluctant to witness and outreach to non-believers will be ineffective.

This Gift in a Team

No matter what the primary focus of a team, there will be many opportunities to share the Gospel, and someone with this gift is most likely to recognize these opportunities and respond.

Typical Strengths

People with this gift tend to be social, secure in their faith, open, and candid. They willingly share their faith, doing so naturally and without much fear of rejection or ridicule.

Potential Pitfalls

At times, people with this gift will become discouraged when they are not seeing a response to their evangelistic efforts. Over time, they may become mechanical in their approach, or too aggressive, and turn off non-believers. Using this gift wisely means talking about your relationship with God, and inviting others to begin one of their own.

Giving (Contributing)

Basic Definition
Giving is a special God-given ability to contribute cheerfully, generously, and regularly to the church and other important ministries, causes, and people in need.

Unique Leadership Contribution
People with this gift manage their personal resources well, contributing as much as possible to people and organizations working to meet needs that are important to them.

This Gift in Scripture
This gift is listed in Romans 12:8 where it is usually translated as "contributing to the needs of others" or "he who gives."

This Gift in Use
People with this gift look for ways to increase their giving to the ministries, causes, and needy individuals they are most committed to supporting. They willingly limit spending on themselves, and they tend to see themselves as partners with those whose work they support. When this gift is missing from the church, ministries will lack the resources required to fulfill their mission.

This Gift in a Team
People who are generous givers are often the best individuals to challenge others to do the same, making them a very effective agent for acquiring the resources the team needs.

Typical Strengths
People with this gift tend to be generous, conscientious, prudent, and resourceful. They look beyond their own needs, and see the benefit of meeting the needs of others.

Potential Pitfalls
Sometimes, people with this gift may be tempted to use their resources to pursue a pet project of their own. Or, they can feel unappreciated if their generosity is not adequately recognized. Using this gift wisely involves acknowledging that all we have comes from God and being grateful for the resources we have that we can use for His glory.

Learning (Knowledge)

Basic Definition

Learning is a special God-given ability to gather, analyze, and share information appropriately with others, leading to greater understanding and insight.

Unique Leadership Contribution

People with this gift research topics of interest to themselves or others, organize their findings systematically, and share what they have learned with others.

This Gift in Scripture

This gift is listed in 1 Corinthians 12:8 where it is usually translated "message of knowledge," "word of knowledge," or "gift of special knowledge."

This Gift in Use

People with this gift are born researchers who love to accumulate and share information. Their unique interest leads them to keep exploring a subject to gain a deeper understanding and more useful information. They enjoy being invited to share their knowledge, helping others quickly gain deeper insight into important matters. When this gift is missing from the church, decisions and plans will be based on inadequate understanding and will eventually fail.

This Gift in a Team

Often people with this gift become a "walking library" of useful information on a wide range of topics crucial to the team's work, as well as the keeper of its learning history.

Typical Strengths

People with this gift tend to be inquisitive, analytical, and proud of their accumulated expertise, with a large appetite for acquiring and sharing information.

Potential Pitfalls

People with this gift need to remember that their latest discovery may not be as exciting to others as to them. They can also fall into the trap of being proud of what they know, even feeling superior to others as a result. The wise use of this gift involves learning to respond to others' self-identified needs for greater understanding in a given area.

Mentoring *(Pastor/Shepherding)*

Basic Definition

Mentoring is a special God-given ability to guide and support individuals or groups as they grow in their faith and in their capacity for ministry.

Unique Leadership Contribution

People with this gift are committed to bringing out the best in others, patiently but firmly nurturing them in their development as whole persons, often on a long-term basis.

This Gift in Scripture

This gift is listed in Ephesians 4:11 where it is usually translated as "pastors."

This Gift in Use

People with this gift willingly accept responsibility for guiding and protecting people who they believe God has entrusted to their care. They identify others' strengths and limitations, and look for timely opportunities to challenge them to grow. Their long-term concern for people makes them highly trusted advisors and coaches. When this gift is missing from the church, people will remain weak in their faith and their Christian walk.

This Gift in a Team

Often people with this gift support a team by supporting its members in an ongoing process of personal and ministry development, both as individuals and as a group.

Typical Strengths

People with this gift tend to be nurturing, growth-minded, and discipleship-oriented. They will look for ways to maximize each person's growth and contribution.

Potential Pitfalls

People with this gift need to be careful about viewing certain people as projects. They may also have difficulty saying no, which can lead to burn-out. Using this gift wisely involves recognizing and maintaining appropriate boundaries, developing healthy relationships that avoid creating dependency between or among those involved.

Organizing (Administration)

Basic Definition

Organizing is a special God–given ability to plan, organize tasks, and follow through so that complex projects are completed efficiently and effectively.

Unique Leadership Contribution

People with this gift ensure the success of a project by clarifying goals, developing detailed plans, delegating tasks, monitoring performance, and managing follow-through.

This Gift in Scripture

This gift is listed in 1 Corinthians 12:28 where it is usually translated as "administration," "governments," or "those who can get others to work together."

This Gift in Use

People with this gift have the capacity to coordinate people, tasks, and resources even in very complex circumstances. Working within the context of the project's goals, they focus on both doing the right things and doing things right. They know how to bring order out of chaos in organizations, always able to see how everything fits together. When this gift is missing from the church, people will become frustrated by confusion, waste, and the inability to get things done.

This Gift in a Team

With so many tasks and people to manage, complexity is a fact of life for most teams. People with this gift develop the systems, processes, and plans to make it all work.

Typical Strengths

People with this gift tend to be highly organized, thorough, clear thinking, and conscientious. They are comfortable with detail and strive for order and harmony.

Potential Pitfalls

People with this gift must be careful not to frustrate other leaders who don't share their enthusiasm for thoroughness and detail. Also, when things aren't going well, they can sometimes seem to be "using people" simply to accomplish tasks. Using this gift wisely involves balancing task requirements and deadlines with people's needs and feelings.

Pioneering (Apostleship)

Basic Definition
Pioneering is a special God-given ability to launch new ventures or lead change, confidently moving forward despite uncertainty or risk.

Unique Leadership Contribution
People with this gift lead the way in spearheading change, testing out new ideas, or leading innovation, often producing breakthroughs in growth or effectiveness.

This Gift in Scripture
This gift is listed in 1 Corinthians 12:28 and Ephesians 4:11 where it is usually translated as "apostles."

This Gift in Use
People with this gift have little fear of the unknown, and an appetite for adventure and even risk. They look for opportunities for growth and change, seeking to move beyond the status quo. Where others get anxious, they get excited. Where others see obstacles, they see opportunities. They always look forward to the next challenge. When this gift is missing from the church, people will find it very difficult to bring about change or start something new.

This Gift in a Team
Even high performing teams can sometimes find themselves in a rut. It takes someone with this gift to stir things up, keep looking ahead, and push for much needed changes.

Typical Strengths
People with this gift tend to be adventurous, risk-taking, adaptable, and confident. Being natural entrepreneurs, they have a make-it-happen approach to the future.

Potential Pitfalls
At times, people with this gift will move too quickly and get ahead of others. They may find themselves disconnected from the supporters they need, sometimes even alienating them. Using this gift wisely involves engaging others in creating a shared vision and in making plans to get there.

Problem-Solving *(Wisdom)*

Basic Definition

Problem-Solving is a special God-given ability to provide practical advice that leads to timely, effective resolution of problems.

Unique Leadership Contribution

People with this gift can often identify simple, practical solutions to problems, helping others find ways to get unstuck and confidently move forward toward their goals.

This Gift in Scripture

This gift is listed in 1 Corinthians 12:8 where it is usually translated as "message of wisdom," "word of wisdom," or "the ability to give wise advice."

This Gift in Use

People with this gift see solutions where others may only see roadblocks. They seem to be able to cut through confusion and conflict and see how to overcome obstacles. They are good at figuring out the best action to take in a given situation. Blessed with an uncommon amount of common sense, they offer practical advice that others willingly follow. When this gift is missing from the church, people may repeat past mistakes or continue doing things the hard way.

This Gift in a Team

Every team runs into problems and needs someone who can offer practical advice to get the team back on track as well as helping the team avoid getting bogged down in the first place.

Typical Strengths

People with this gift will tend to be logical, sensible, observant, and highly practical. They will see options others miss and carefully choose the most effective way forward.

Potential Pitfalls

People with this gift may be tempted to hold back from sharing their insights until someone invites them to do so, perhaps because they have learned that others are not always open to advice. Using this gift wisely involves learning how to share important insights and suggestions in ways that others can understand and embrace them.

Speaking Out *(Prophet)*

Basic Definition
Speaking Out is a special God-given ability to declare God's truth boldly and publicly for the purpose of correction or instruction.

Unique Leadership Contribution
People with this gift challenge others to change their behavior by speaking out clearly and convincingly about right and wrong, even where it may be unpopular.

This Gift in Scripture
This gift is listed in Romans 12:6, 1 Corinthians 12:10, 28, and Ephesians 4:11 where it is usually translated as "prophesying," "prophets," or "ability to prophesy."

This Gift in Use
People with this gift are especially attuned both to God's principles and to what is really going on in the world. They look for the right time and place to share what they feel must be said to influence others. They tend to see issues that others fail to see and feel compelled to speak out. When this gift is missing from the church, people can lose touch with God's heart and his will.

This Gift in a Team
Often people with this gift support a team by serving as a kind of "moral compass," challenging others to live up to biblical standards of right and wrong.

Typical Strengths
People with this gift will tend to be individualistic, opinionated, outspoken, and determined. They will see situations and issues in very clear, black-and-white terms.

Potential Pitfalls
At times, people with this gift will be difficult to be around because of their strong need to speak out, which may be perceived as overly judgmental and critical of others. Using this gift wisely involves being compassionate toward others and having a genuine desire to motivate others to change rather than a need simply to point out where they are wrong.

Supporting *(Helps)*

Basic Definition

Supporting is a special God-given ability to provide practical, behind-the-scenes help that frees others to accomplish more than they might otherwise be capable of achieving.

Unique Leadership Contribution

People with this gift usually like to work behind the scenes, supporting the work of others, cheerfully finding and doing small things that need doing, often without being asked.

This Gift in Scripture

This gift is listed in Romans 12:7 and 1 Corinthians 12:28 where it is usually translated as "helps," "serving," "ministry," "forms of assistance," or "those able to help others."

This Gift in Use

People with this gift take pride in doing the seemingly small tasks others sometimes consider mundane or routine. They appreciate how their service frees others to focus on "higher level" tasks. When this gift is missing from the church, leaders can become bogged down by details or worn out from trying to do everything alone.

This Gift in a Team

No one gets to do the glamorous work all of the time, but those with this gift willingly take on the more routine tasks, making it possible for high-performing teams to excel.

Typical Strengths

People with this gift tend to be flexible, easy-going, dependable, and humble. They take pride in serving others faithfully without concern for recognition or honor.

Potential Pitfalls

People with this gift often find it difficult to say no, causing them to over-commit, which leads to a loss of balance in their lives. Some also come to depend on what they do for others for their self-worth. Using this gift wisely involves recognizing that God values people for who they are, not what they do, and by maintaining a healthy, balanced life.

Teaching *(Teacher)*

Basic Definition
Teaching is a special God-given ability to organize and clearly communicate knowledge and skills to others, and to motivate them to master and apply what they are learning.

Unique Leadership Contribution
People with this gift identify the knowledge and skills others need to learn, and use creative approaches to help them learn willingly and effectively.

This Gift in Scripture
This gift is listed in Romans 12:7, 1 Corinthians 12:28, and Ephesians 4:11 where it is usually translated as "teaching" or "teacher."

This Gift in Use
People with this gift focus on helping others develop their knowledge and skill, including their knowledge of Christian principles. They begin by understanding the learning needs of others, and then look for teachable moments to engage people in creative, enjoyable learning activities that lead to knowledge and skill improvement. When this gift is missing from the church, people will not grow in depth of faith or capacity for ministry.

This Gift in a Team
Often people with this gift have the best feel for the strengths and limitations of the team. They often can tell what others need to learn and how to help them learn it.

Typical Strengths
People with this gift will usually be skilled at organizing ideas, creative, and enthusiastic. They have a special knack for making difficult concepts easier to learn.

Potential Pitfalls
The most common shortcoming of people with this gift is their tendency to over-teach, presenting too much content and not enough opportunity for reflection, review, and experimenting with application. Using this gift wisely involves continually "checking in" with the learners and adjusting to their motivation, pace, and learning style.

Partnering with youth workers to develop students into leaders.

It's our belief that the church is one generation away from a leadership void and if we don't intentionally develop leaders, the church will struggle. To that end, we developed the LeaderTreks model for leadership development. We apply this model to all the resources and training events we offer.

LeaderTreks comes alongside of youth workers providing:

- Leadership training events for students

- Leadership resources

- Leadership driven mission and wilderness trips

- Youth Worker Training

Check out our website at www.leadertreks.org

Developing Leaders to Fulfill the Great Commission

877-502-0699